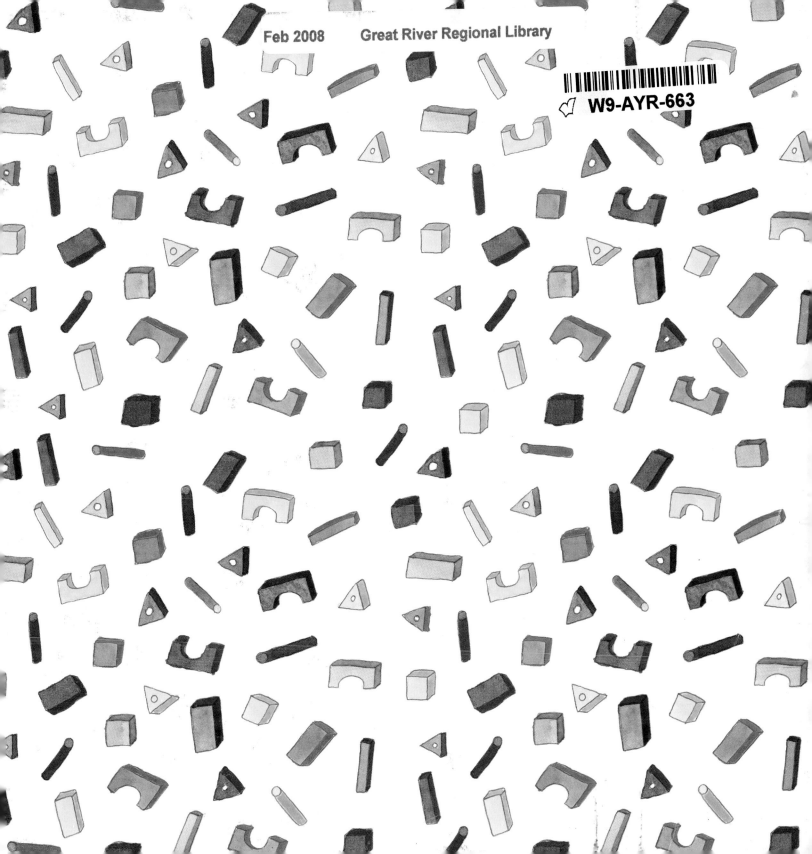

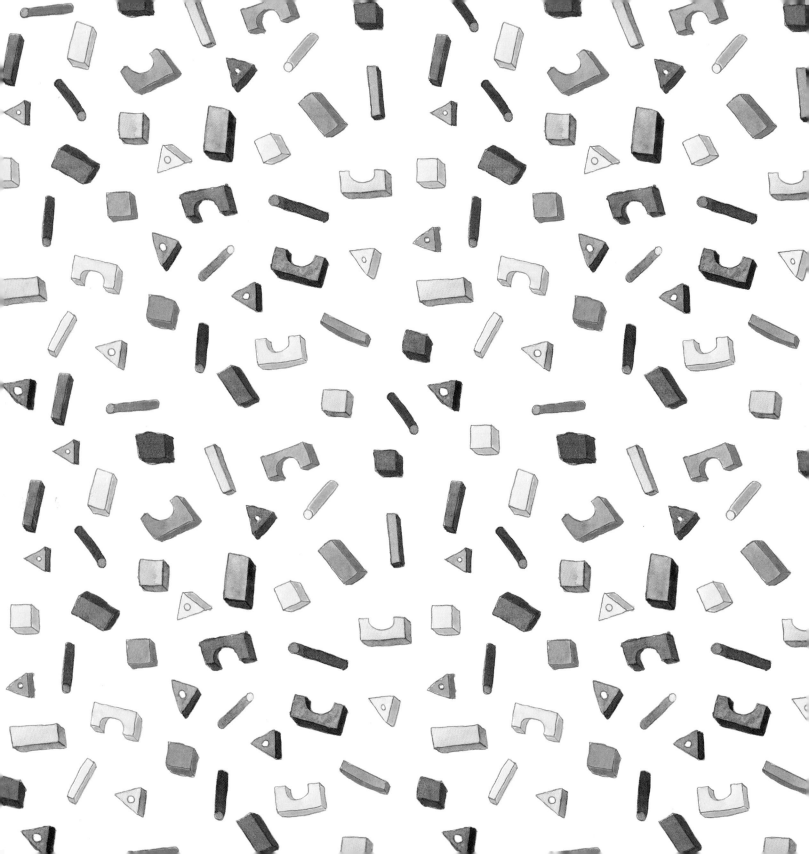

Emily Post

Emily's Sharing and Caring Book

By Cindy Post Senning, Ed.D., and Peggy Post

Illustrated by Leo Landry

Collins

An Imprint of HarperCollinsPublishers

Collins is an imprint of HarperCollins Publishers.

Emily's Sharing and Caring Book
Text copyright © 2008 by Cindy Post Senning and Peggy Post
Illustrations copyright © 2008 by Leo Landry
Manufactured in China.

Library of Congress Cataloging-in-Publication Data
Senning, Cindy Post.
    Emily's sharing and caring book / by Cindy Post Senning, Ed.D., and Peggy Post ;
illustrated by Leo Landry.
        p.   cm.
    ISBN-10: 0-06-111697-1 (trade bdg.) — ISBN 978-0-06-111697-1 (trade bdg.)
    ISBN 0-06-111698-X (lib. bdg.) — ISBN 978-0-06-111698-8 (lib. bdg.)
    1. Etiquette for children and teenagers. 2. Sharing—Juvenile literature. 3. Caring—
Juvenile literature. I. Post, Peggy, 1945– II. Landry, Leo. III. Title.
BJ1857.C5S42 2008   2006102927
395.1'22—dc22   CIP
                                                                      AC

Typography by Jeanne L. Hogle
1 2 3 4 5 6 7 8 9 10
❖
First Edition

Dedicated to the toddlers we have experienced and loved:
Casey, Jeep, Peter, Paul, Danny, Willy, Anna, and Lizzie
—C.P.S. and P.P.

For Debbie and Andy
—L.L.

Shall I tell you how?

By sharing

and caring!

It's easy to share with others.

Do you know how to take turns?

That's sharing.

There are lots of ways to share:

You can share toys,

or share food.

You can share time

or a good mood.

It's easy to show you care for others.

Do you think about others and what you can do to make other people feel good?

That's caring!

There are lots of times to show you care:

when someone is hurt,

or when someone is sad,

or when you want to make
someone feel special.

But the real secret about sharing
and caring is that they can do more
than make others smile.

They can make you smile, too.

Sharing and caring

make everyone happy.

Dear Parents,

Wouldn't it be wonderful if all that was required to have children be kind, respectful, and considerate was to teach a set of manners, or social skills, as we call them? Children *do* need to learn the "magic" words, basic table manners, greeting and introduction skills, and all the other manners we think of when we talk about etiquette. That's for sure! But etiquette is about more than manners; it's also about building good relationships. *So* children need to learn the behaviors that help them act in ways that are respectful, considerate, and honest—the fundamental principles of etiquette.

While these principles are *too* difficult for a toddler to understand, a child this age *is* developmentally ready to learn some basic behaviors that will help build strong relationships. Most three-year-olds, for example, are able to understand that *sharing* and *caring* make other people feel good. They know this because they can see the smiles that sharing and caring bring.

A smile is concrete. Your toddler can see the results of positive behavior in your smile. And he or she can identify with the feeling he or she gets from making someone else smile—it makes him or her smile, too. It will take much patience, repetition, and good modeling on your part to teach your toddler to share and care. It's well worth it, though. You will be raising a respectful, kind, considerate child!

—Cindy and Peggy

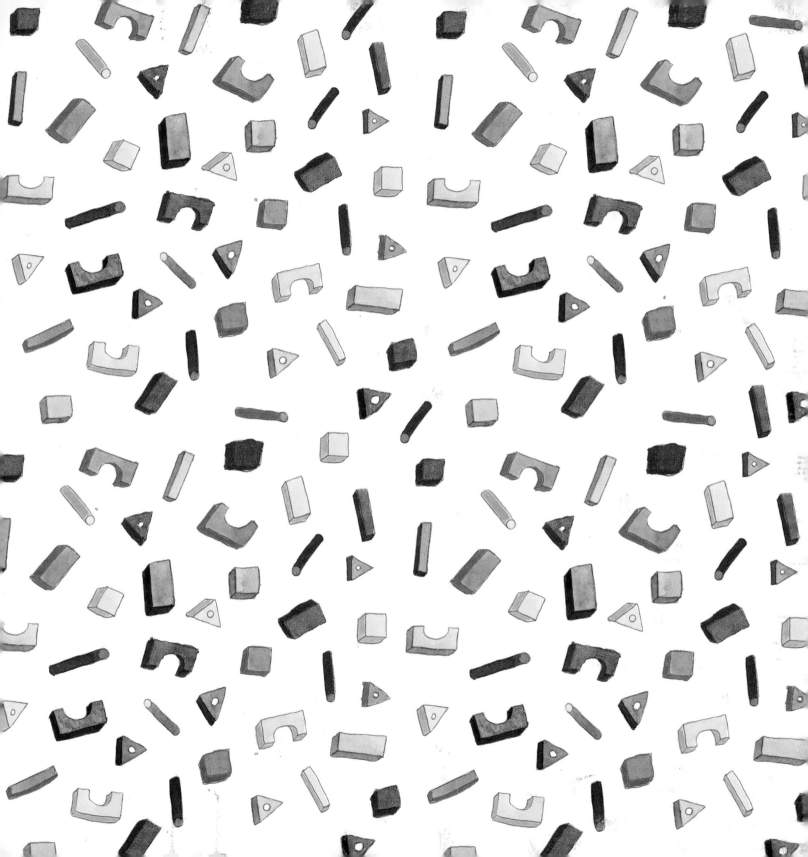